BIBLE STORIES
GIANT COLORING BOOK

Modern Publishing
A Division of Unisystems, Inc.
New York, New York 10022
Series UPC: 47100
17995 – July 2009

The
Old

Testament

The

Creation

1n the beginning, God created the Heavens and the Earth, and all the wonderful creatures that live there.

God created Adam to rule over all the creatures of the Earth.

Eve was created from Adam's rib, to keep him company.
They lived happily in the Garden of Eden.

But the serpent tempted Eve to eat the forbidden fruit.

Eve disobeyed God and gave the fruit to Adam.

Adam and Eve were driven out of the Garden of Eden.

Noah

and

the Flood

Adam and Eve's descendants sinned against God. He wanted to punish them. But he chose one righteous man to save. He told Noah to build an ark and gather animals of every kind.

Then God sent a huge storm to flood the Earth.

The animals entered the ark, two by two.

It rained for forty days. At last, Noah sent the dove out looking for land. When it returned with an olive branch in its mouth, he knew the flood was over.

Ｇod sent a rainbow as a sign that he would never again
destroy the Earth

The Tower of Babel

God's people wanted to build a city with a tower high enough to reach the heavens. But God was angry at their pride. He made them all speak different languages, so they could not understand each other. The city was never finished.

Abraham and

Isaac

Abraham was the Lord's faithful servant. God chose him to found the Hebrew nation.

Abraham wanted a son, but his wife, Sarah, had grown old.
Then the Lord came to Abraham with two angels and promised
him a son. Sarah laughed at the prophecy, but it came true.
She had a son and named him Isaac.

God told Abraham to sacrifice Isaac. Abraham loved Isaac,
but he loved God more. He led Isaac to the altar.

But God rewarded Abraham's obedience. He sent a ram to be sacrificed in Isaac's place.

The Story

of Lot

The people of Sodom sinned. God sent two angels to destroy the city. But a good man named Lot lived there. The angels warned him to flee before the city was destroyed.

Lot took his wife and fled. But his wife looked back and was turned into a pillar of salt.

The Coat

of Many Colors

Jacob gave his son, Joseph, a beautiful coat of many colors.

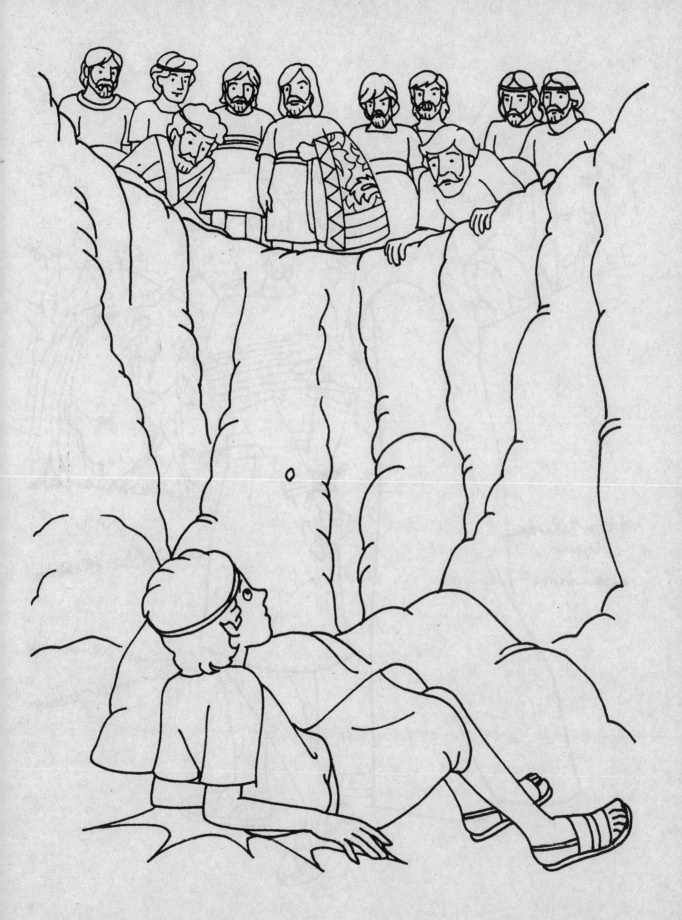

Joseph's brothers were jealous. They threw Joseph into a pit.

$\mathcal{T}$hen they sold him into slavery in Egypt.

The Lord gave Joseph the power to interpret dreams.
He became the Pharaoh's favorite servant.

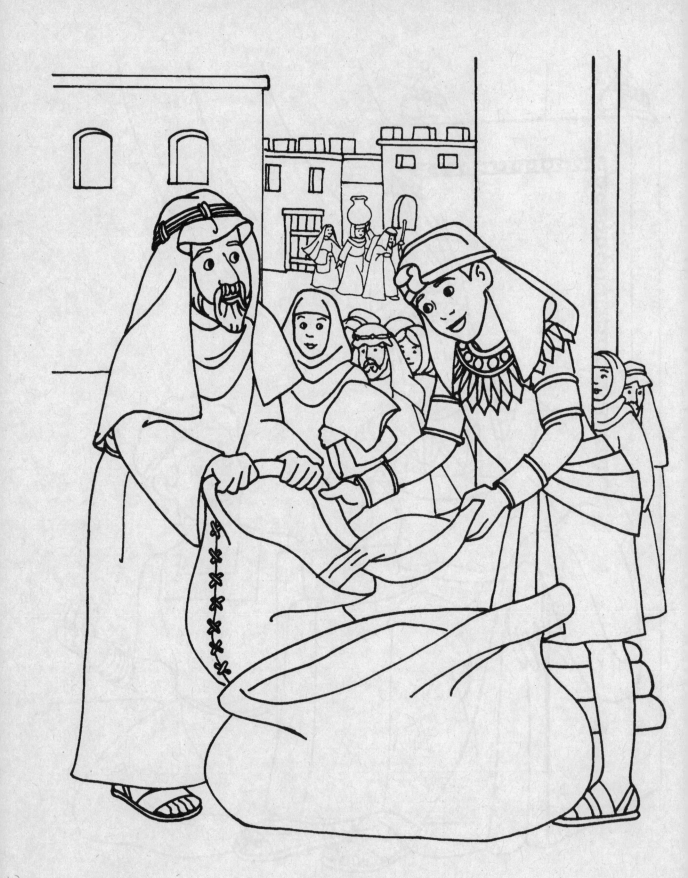

Joseph warned the Egyptians that a famine was coming.
He saved the people from starvation.

Joseph's brothers were suffering from the famine. They came to him to buy grain. When they recognized him, they were afraid, but he forgave them.

Moses Leads

the Hebrews

Pharaoh ordered all the Hebrew babies to be drowned in the Nile. But Moses' mother hid him in the reeds. Pharaoh's daughter found him and took him in.

God spoke to Moses from a burning bush, calling him to lead the Israelites out of slavery in Egypt.

Moses asked Pharaoh to let his people go, but Pharaoh refused.
So Moses asked God to bring a plague of frogs on the
house of Egypt.

Still, Pharaoh would not relent, so Moses brought
a plague of snakes to Egypt.

Then he brought a plague of hail, but Pharaoh would not set the Hebrews free.

God was angry at the Egyptians. He vowed to kill all their firstborn. But he told the Jews to put a sign on their doors, and he spared their children.

At last, Pharaoh agreed to let the Israelites go.
Moses struck the Red Sea, and it parted to let them pass!

ut Pharaoh sent his army to stop them. When Moses saw the Egyptians coming, he stretched out his hand, and the waters rushed back, drowning the army.

The Israelites had to cross the desert to get to the Promised Land. The journey was hard, and they had nothing to eat. Then God sent manna and quails from Heaven.

Ｇod told Moses to strike a rock, and water
poured out for the people to drink.

The Amalekites attacked the Hebrews, but Moses held up his magic staff, and the Hebrews won the battle.

The Ten Commandments

Moses climbed Mount Sinai to receive the Ten Commandments of God. They were engraved on stone tablets.

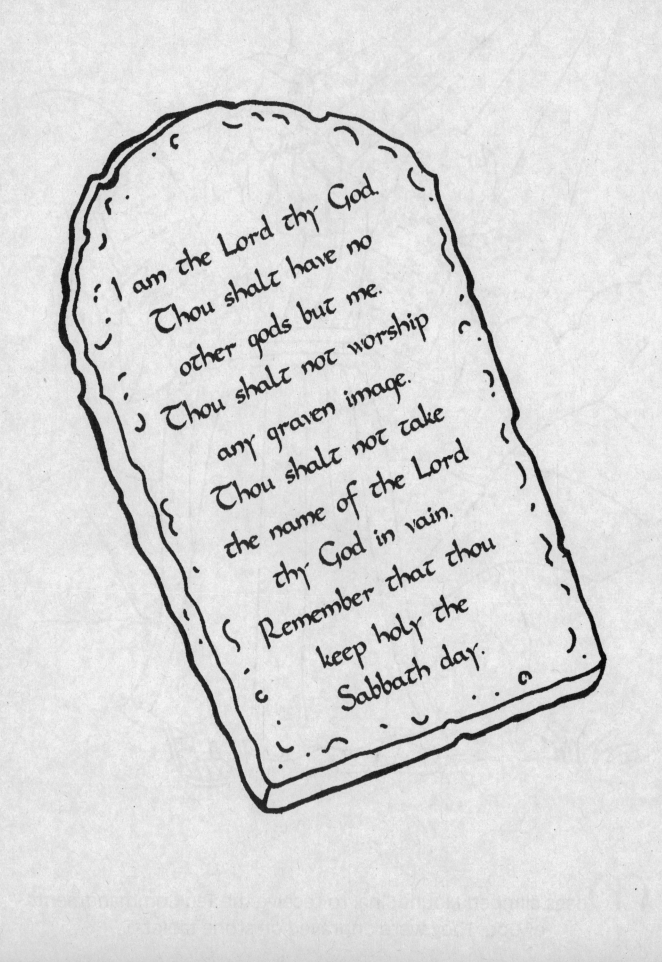

The Golden

Calf

While Moses was away, his brother Aaron made a golden statue of a calf. The people forgot about God and worshipped the calf.

When Moses came back, he was angry. He broke the tablets.
But God gave the people new tablets, and they built a
gold-covered chest to hold them.

Balaam's

Donkey

When the Israelites came to the Promised Land, the King of Moab was afraid of them. He sent a man named Balaam to curse them. But God sent an angel to block his path. Balaam's donkey saw the angel and would not pass.

Balaam beat his donkey, until at last the donkey turned and asked
why Balaam was beating her. Then Balaam saw the angel and
blessed the Israelites.

The Walls of Jericho

At last, Joshua led the people into the Promised Land. When they came to the walled city of Jericho, God told them to march around the city seven times. When they blew their trumpets, the walls collapsed, and the Israelites marched in.

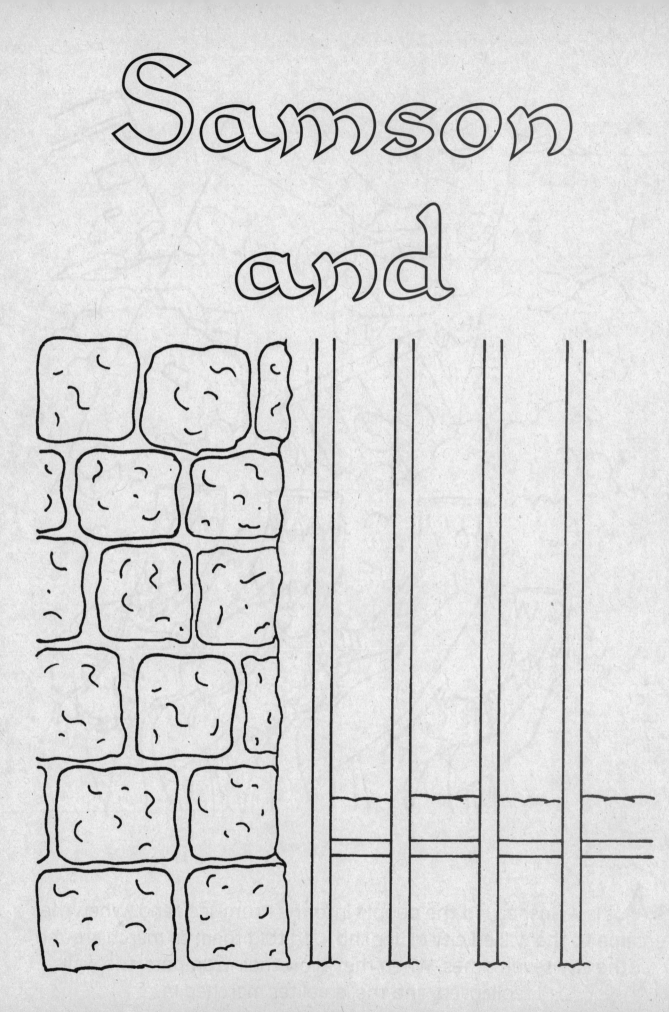

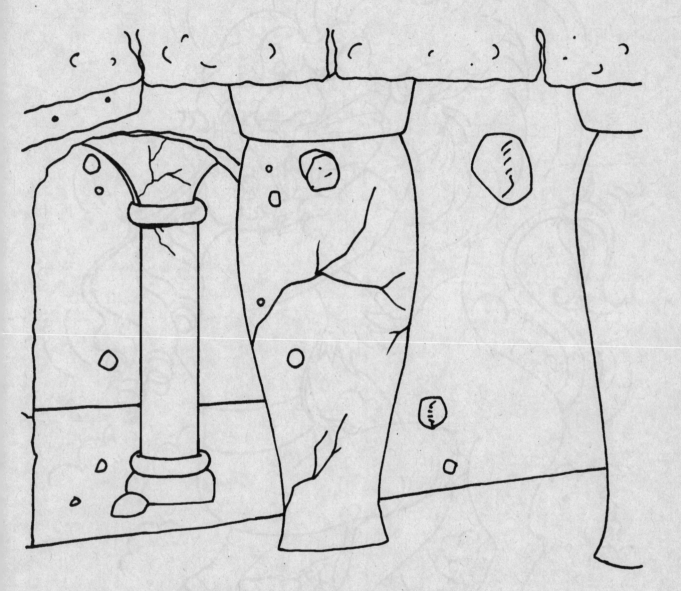

Delilah

Samson had amazing strength from God. He was chosen to
lead the Hebrews against the Philistines.

But Samson fell in love with the beautiful Delilah. She tricked him into telling her the secret of his strength: it came from his hair. While he slept, Delilah cut his hair.

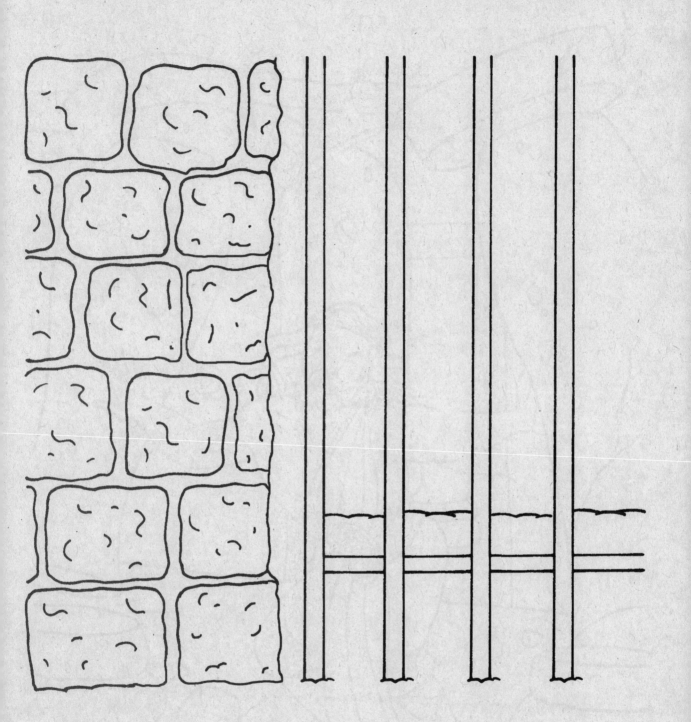

Samson was blinded and thrown into prison.
Night and day he prayed to God to restore his strength.

At last, Samson's prayers were answered.
His hair grew back, and he destroyed the Philistines'
temple in God's name.

David
and

Goliath

Goliath, a giant, led the Philistine army. The Israelites were afraid to fight him. But David, a young shepherd boy, was not afraid. "God will be with me," he said.

With his slingshot, David defeated Goliath.

David became the King of Israel.

He wrote beautiful psalms praising God.

The Twenty-Third Psalm

The Lord is my shepherd;
I shall not want.

He maketh me to lie down
in green pastures.

He leadeth me beside the
still waters.

He restoreth my soul.

Yea, though I walk through the
valley of the shadow of death,

I will fear no evil, for
Thou art with me.

Thy rod and Thy staff, they
comfort me.

Thou preparest a table before me
in the presence of mine enemies.

Thou annointest my head with oil.

My cup runneth over.

Surely goodness and mercy shall
follow me all the days of my life.

And I will dwell in the house of
the Lord forever.

David's son, Solomon, became king when he was just a boy. God told him to ask for anything he desired, and Solomon asked for the wisdom to rule fairly. God was pleased with this unselfish request. He made Solomon the wisest ruler who ever lived.

Once, two women were arguing over a baby. "Let the baby be cut in half, and half given to each," said Solomon. The real mother said, "Give the baby to the other woman, but let him live!" Then Solomon knew this was the true mother, and he gave the baby to her.

The

Prophets

Elijah was a great prophet. At the end of his days,
he was carried up to heaven on a whirlwind.

Elisha was the next great prophet. Naaman, a great warrior, came to ask him to heal his leprosy.

Elisha told Naaman to wash seven times in the river Jordan. Naaman went to the river and was cured.

King Nebuchadnezzar commanded everyone to worship a golden statue. But Shadrach, Meshach, and Abed-nego refused. The king had them thrust into a furnace, but an angel protected them. When Nebuchadnezzar saw this, he set them free.

Daniel in the

Lion's
Den

King Darius passed a law that said no one could worship anything except him. But Daniel would not stop worshipping God, so he was thrown to the lions. Darius was sorry about this law. "I hope your God will save you," he told Daniel.

Daniel prayed to God, and the lions did not hurt him. Darius was amazed. He ordered all his people to worship Daniel's God.

Jonah and the

Whale

God was angry with the people of Nineveh. He called Jonah to deliver his message. But Jonah was afraid to go to Nineveh. He got on a ship to escape from God's command.

God sent a storm to stop the ship. Jonah confessed that God was angry at him. He told the sailors to throw him into the sea.

God sent a great fish to swallow Jonah so he would not drown. In the belly of the fish, Jonah repented and promised to serve God.

God forgave Jonah and made the fish spit him out onto the shore.

Jonah took God's message to Nineveh.

Psalm 100

Shout for joy to the LORD,
all the earth.

Worship the LORD with gladness;
come before him with joyful songs.

Know that the LORD is God.
It is he who made us,
and we are his; we are his people,
the sheep of his pasture.

Enter his gates with thanksgiving
and his courts with praise;
give thanks to him and
praise his name.

For the LORD is good and
his love endures forever;
his faithfulness continues
through all generations.

Psalm 1

Blessed is the man
who does not walk
in the counsel of the wicked
or stand in the way of sinners
or sit in the seat of mockers.

But his delight is in
the law of the LORD,
and on his law he
meditates day and night.

He is like a tree planted by
streams of water,
which yields its fruit in season
and whose leaf does not wither.

Whatever he does prospers.
Not so the wicked!
They are like chaff
that the wind blows away.

Therefore the wicked will not
stand in the judgment,
nor sinners in the assembly
of the righteous.

For the LORD watches over
the way of the righteous,
but the way of
the wicked will perish.

Psalm 130

Out of the depths I cry to you,
O LORD;
O Lord, hear my voice.

Let your ears be attentive
to my cry for mercy.

If you, O LORD,
kept a record of sins,
O Lord, who could stand?

But with you there is forgiveness;
therefore you are feared.

I wait for the LORD,
my soul waits,

and in his word I put my hope.
My soul waits for the Lord
more than watchmen wait
for the morning,
more than watchmen wait
for the morning.

O Israel, put your hope
in the LORD,
for with the LORD
is unfailing love
and with him is full redemption.

He himself will redeem Israel
from all their sins.